BEYOND FRONTLINE
EXCELLENCE

BEYOND FRONTLINE
EXCELLENCE

Spirituality in Business for Frontline Professionals

ANCHAL ANDREWS

PARTRIDGE

A Penguin Random House Company

To order additional copies of this book, contact
Toll Free 800 101 2657 (Singapore)
Toll Free 1 800 81 7340 (Malaysia)
orders.singapore@partridgepublishing.com

www.partridgepublishing.com/singapore

Contents

Acknowledgements

There are many brilliant people to thank for this work. Amongst them are my family, to whom I dedicate this book, with a special thank you to my father, Dr Sudhir Andrews (DLitt), for his inspiration during the editorial phase; my mother, Mrs Roma Andrews, for her unconditional support; and my brother, Mr Aakash Andrews, for his consistent belief in my abilities.

Chapter 1

Beyond Frontline Excellence – The Concept

This book brings a new approach to business relationships with present and future customers. It takes customer service beyond excellence by integrating conventional practices with spirituality. I call this approach *Beyond Frontline Excellence*.

Customer service comes from the heart, and so does spirituality. They have a symbiotic relationship that can offer a 'wow' customer experience. The main customer expectation is a memorable experience that is actualised through an organisation's values as expressed by that business's representatives. These values, in part, determine a customer's loyalty. Customers are not merely looking for purchases anymore; they want memorable buying experiences, whether business-to-business or business-to-consumer. This can be achieved through spirituality when dealing with customers.

Spirituality unblocks any reservations a customer may have towards products, services, or businesses. It harvests the good in everybody when dealing with each other. Providing honest information will be the future order of business to attract a discerning and well-informed customer. This book is written to bring both aspects together– spirituality and customer service – by broadening the individual's sense of identity to reflect business values with professionalism.

It is vital to note that the Information Age has made the customer a king. Just as the Industrial Revolution brought about the Industrial Age, the Digital Revolution brought the Information Age. During the Industrial Age businesses decided what kinds of products customers should have, and they controlled information and supply flow of these products. They moved their products through a network of distributors and retailers who became the cornerstone of all interactions with customers. Customers depended on them for the availability of the products and the information about them. In the Information Age customers have direct access, with the click of a button, to the best products in the world and information about them. Businesses, therefore, are forced to move from a sales cycle to a buying cycle, placing the customer in a position as king. The Information Age made the marketplace truly global, and most competition became fierce, with access to customers and businesses across the globe, and in this way relationships decide the survival of a business. In the past customers enquired about a company's products by asking, 'Is the product useful?'; 'Is the product desirable?'; 'Is the product usable?' Today, customers enquire about company values by asking, 'Is the company easy to deal with?'; 'Is the company enjoyable to deal with?'; 'Does the company meet needs?'

Unfortunately, business and politics are strange bedfellows that suffocate the common working professional in their crossfire, negatively impacting the ultimate customer experience today. The two taint the perceptions of business leaders, who make biased decisions which are not conducive to business efficiency, effectiveness, and survival, especially in relation to the customer. Therefore, for the overall health and survival of a business, the professional self, and the society of today and tomorrow, it is essential to integrate something more to give memorable buying experiences. This 'something more' are the values that bolster spirituality. Businesses are not physical, inanimate structures but rather the *people* working within these structures – especially the frontline staff, who provide the ultimate customer experience on behalf of the business. The frontline staff need to go beyond rehearsed responses to customers, to get the cutting edge over their competition.

To do this, individuals must know their potential and power intrinsically. This can be done by identifying the role of spirituality in everyday living and then bringing it to customer service. But what is the spiritual self?

The Spiritual Self

The spiritual self is the core of an individual with a unique cluster of qualities that cannot be replicated in another person. The cluster is unique because it is a combination of inborn qualities, genetic qualities, and culturally learned qualities. This implies that we cannot apply one common method of customer service to everyone.

The English word 'spirit' is from the Latin *spiritus,* meaning 'breath'. When we breathe, we come alive. Usually with life comes human consciousness. Human anatomy is tied to human consciousness; therefore, as our physical breathing patterns change, so do our thought patterns, and vice versa.

Dr Martin Kramar, a psychologist, member of the American Psychological Association, and member of British Psychological Society, said,

> We learn to voluntarily control our autonomic nervous system via sympathetic (anxiety and stress-fight/flight response to situation) and parasympathetic (relaxation-composure to situation) activation. The right hemisphere of the human brain which is responsible for relaxation is activated by [the] parasympathetic nervous system. The left hemisphere which is responsible for reasoning is activated by

the sympathetic nervous system. Balance between the right and a left hemisphere is needed to attain psycho-physiological equilibrium concerning sensitivity and reasoning for better harmony.

Therefore, by being conscious of our breathing, we can influence our thoughts and feelings. This brings our spiritual self into play. For example, we can achieve awareness of our breathing through meditation, reading, any form of exercise, yoga, prayer, and so on to get in touch with our spiritual selves. In this book we are not concerned with the science of this; instead, we are concerned with the effects.

Therefore, in essence, spirituality is affirmed meaningful activities that lead to a reformed self to attain perfection. Affirmed meaningful activities are those things we do within ourselves to recognise our talents, influence our thoughts and feelings, monitor our breathing, be conscious of our physical selves through self-control to strike a balance, and so on. We do them outside ourselves to nurture our talents through training and education, to meditate, to positively modify behaviour, and to care for our health through meaningful recreational activities. These will lead to fulfilment, and one can strive for perfection.

Perfection is the translation of absolute ideas to reality. An absolute idea is the blueprint in our minds for action. For example, excellence and consistency are two pure potential 'absolute ideas' as ideal blueprints in our minds that await action. Absolute ideas can be converted to everyday living experiences. Excellence and consistency can be converted by frontline professionals to customers, who are king.

There is a universe within us that we perceive as truth. Similarly, there is a universe outside us that we perceive as fact and therefore also as truth. The individual 'truth' of internal perceptions – as much as the truth of external facts of both the frontline professional and the customer – meet to create the augmented customer experience. The challenge for a frontline professional is to understand the internal truths and external facts of the customer that defines his or her experience. The professional should try to align them for a positive interaction and a meaningful experience. For example, inventions come from a blueprint in the mind, which is 'truth' before it is transformed into reality.

Inventions need the materials and methods to translate the blueprint into reality. The customer relies on the invention. Suppose the invention is a glass for drinking water that you want to sell to the customer. As a demonstration you might set up a transparent glass of water. If one accepted that truth represented by untainted perceptions exists, then the truth is there, a transparent glass of water. It would not matter whether it was half full or half empty, because the invention serves the purpose of holding water. This type of realisation is brought about with the emergence of soft skills.

Diagram 1:

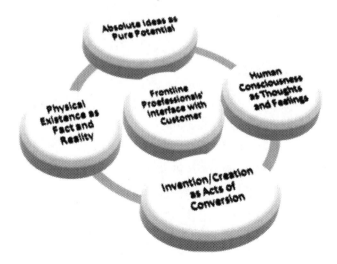

Chapter 2

Emergence of Soft Skills

Emotional intelligence is the ability to recognize one's own and other people's emotions, to discriminate between different feelings and label them appropriately, and to use emotional information to guide thinking and behaviour.

Andrew Coleman, *A Dictionary of Psychology*

Influenced by the writing of Dale Carnegie, I assert that going beyond frontline excellence starts with personal attributes of individuals, such as a person's soft skills, which are observable. 'Soft skills' is a term often associated with a person's EQ (emotional intelligence quotient). This comprises the cluster of an individual's personality traits, social graces, verbal and non-verbal communication, rules of language, prevailing personal habits, ability to be friendly, capacity to manage people, leadership, and all those areas that characterise relationships with other people in terms of translating emotional intelligence to behaviour. Soft skills assist the individual in harmonising with people in any environment. These can be learnt whilst retaining the core of an individual.

Emotional intelligence is the key to bringing together spirituality and customer service within a business. For example, I believe morality is rooted in spirituality, whilst soft skills are used in customer interaction; both are nurtured by emotional intelligence.

In this context morality is defined as the human character and personal description derived from the Greek word *ethos*, alongside customs and manners as derived from the Latin word *mores*. The terms 'morality' and 'soft skills' must come together, since soft skills may also be used to manipulate people, which is not the intention frontline professionals should have. Adaptive behaviours by frontline professionals are acceptable when true to the authentic expectations of the customer. The basic premise of this book is to bring in spirituality whilst dealing with people, to bring soft skills to as close to a level of perfection as possible.

For businesses, hard skills – which are skills that are easy to measure and pertain to specific work abilities – are required for 50 per cent of jobs done, whilst the remaining 50 per cent require soft skills, which are usually harder to quantify and less tangible. Without soft skills 50 per cent of these jobs will not realise their potential. Businesses have to adapt quickly to the customers' changing needs and dispositions to survive in a global competition. This evolution puts control in the hands of the customers, making relationships with them vital. Clearly, soft skills matter more now than ever before, since these strongly influence business success. Any experience with a business is measured, rated, and evaluated by the customer, who will then decide whether he or she will repeat business or even refer the business and its products to other potential customers. Customers now demand totally different experiences that are lifetime experiences in excellence and consistency. To achieve this, businesses have to overcome certain hurdles.

Hurdles to Meeting Customer Expectations

Many companies claim to create unique experiences for customers by investing in various types of systems and novel behaviours but still have difficulties in holding their customers. So what's missing?

Why is it difficult to retain them? Customers want to interact with a business in more ways than before, as shown in diagram 2:

Customers expect excellence and consistency in their experience at every touchpoint of a business. Touchpoints are a point of contact or interaction, especially between a business and its customers or consumers, such as showrooms, websites, call centres, workshops, field services, social media, print contents, etc. Customers view each and every interaction as doing business with the company. To earn their business and loyalty the company has to adapt to the new ways customers want to do business with it, and not the other way around. This puts a high premium on abilities to provide consistent engagement across any channel at any time. Therefore, the qualities of individuals at each touchpoint require excellence and consistency in responses from individuals representing the business.

Unfortunately, each touchpoint lives in a silo, each with its own systems and responses. The inconsistent responses to customers' needs create frustration. For example, inconsistency in delivery timelines; uncorrelated product features, advantages, and benefits; commitments made without determining whether these commitments are even possible; or promotions being disclosed as discounts with free add-on products or the promotion is disclosed as costs built in to meet profit margins.

There can be any number of inconsistencies in business information flow because each touchpoint lives in a silo. Inconsistencies can pertain to process, structure, technical skills, and soft knowledge. Businesses occasionally create systems and training for each touchpoint that are in isolation from each other. This results in fractured consistency and continuity. Customers have to repeat themselves, creating frustration.

Each touchpoint acknowledges the transaction history prior to any interaction with the customer. The lack of a seamless dialogue between the customers and the individuals representing the business creates customer frustration, which results in lost sales and decreased satisfactions.

For example, an automotive company identified SSI scores (sales satisfaction index) from November 2014 to May 2015. Training programs were held in various batches for the company frontline and management staff from November 2014 to January 2015. At the end of the sessions, sales and satisfaction of services had shot up dramatically as identified by a series of surveys conducted by the company with their esteemed customers. The survey targeted areas in which the participants were trained and developed. Note the progress by change of percentages in the graph - diagram 3:

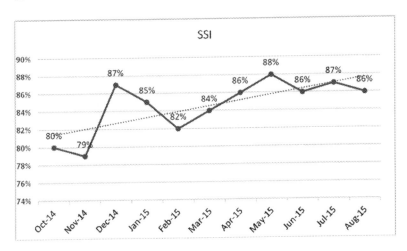

- The sales satisfaction index (SSI) in 2014 averaged around 79–80 per cent.
- Process and soft-skills training was conducted between November 2014 and January 2015.
- SSI scores jumped to 87 per cent in January 2015, and has trended to 85 per cent in 2015, an increase of 5 per cent.
- Customer service retention (as defined as the percentage of customers who continue to retain their services) has shown a significant improvement.
- Retention rates have gone up by more than 10 per cent.
- The reason for increased retention was implementation of better reminder and follow-up process and overall improvements in service.

Businesses have attempted to keep pace with changing customer expectations in how they wish to interact. New customer service management positions have been created by the current generation, and internal solutions have been implemented to optimize each new channel – the appointment of customer experience specialists, in-house training academies, buddy systems (mentors) on the job, etc. However, these attempts have been isolated from other interaction points. The challenge is to harmonize all touchpoint responses so as to create a unified response of excellence and consistency, as indicated in the example above.

The customer journey has become more complex. The customer buying journey often starts long before the customer ever engages with a company. Easy access to the experiences of other customers through social media; product information, and service reviews on the Internet; and word-of-mouth referrals result in customers being much more knowledgeable about the business's products, prices, and services in advance. This means everyone will need to be given the same information across all business touchpoints to attract and retain the best customers. This includes knowledge of the business's values.

Improving relationships will improve loyalty. For example, in the hospitality industry (part of the service sector), a study on a chain of restaurants has shown that improving relationships has improved customer loyalty; relationships were improved by businesses displaying basic values through specific communication skills and supplying their customers with lifetime experiences.

These seven basic value-displaying communication skills, as described by Nancy Friedman, customer service expert and 'Telephone Doctor', are

- empathy: having the capacity for understanding; being aware of and sensitive to the feelings, thoughts, and experiences of a customer;
- enthusiasm: bringing an observable high level of energy or interest to a project or situation;
- responsibility: living up to previously agreed-upon commitments;
- balance: having the capacity to successfully satisfy the customer while taking into account the resources and needs of your organization

- adaptability: having the flexibility to effectively deal with different types of customers and situations;
- ownership: possessing the commitment to solve a problem or ability to steer it toward someone who will; and
- resiliency: having the ability to bounce back from adversity.

Business representatives were asked to share experiences where they have displayed these skills:

Participant 1 avoided serious grievances from recurring; she displayed empathy.

Participant 2 corrected a wrong order; she displayed resiliency.

Participant 3 owned the prevailing concern with her customer; she displayed ownership

Participant 4 handled a customer's grievance; she displayed empathy.

Participant 5 substituted for a colleague's absence as a gesture for team work; he displayed responsibility and adaptability

Participant 6 equally evaluated the customer's concern and the business; she displayed balance.

Participant 7 met the needs of the customer while staying within the rules of the company; she displayed balance.

Participant 8 even as evident in her participation in a training course to improve skills, she displayed resiliency.

Participant 9 corrected her mistake while dealing with a customer who did not speak the same language and whose order was replaced by another customer's order; she displayed ownership and resiliency.

Participant 10 substituted for a manager on leave; he displayed responsibility.

Participant 11 resolved escalations; he displayed ownership.

Participant 12 bounced back from adverse issues at the workplace; he displayed resiliency.

Participant 13 cared for her customer by going the extra mile; she displayed empathy.

Participant 14 took on work challenges at the managerial level; he displayed responsibility.

Participant 15 was passionate about his work and supported the manager; he displayed enthusiasm and responsibility.

Participant 16 convinced prospects to dine at the restaurant; she displayed enthusiasm.

Participant 17 expressed interest in expanding her knowledge base to serve customers; she displayed adaptability and enthusiasm.

Participant 18 apologized for issues in food packaging and assured there would be solutions moving forward; she displayed empathy, enthusiasm, and ownership.

Participant 19 showed concern for his internal and external customers; he displayed empathy and enthusiasm.

Therefore, customers know their value and demand exclusive attention at all times. Once customers become fans of the business, they share an emotional bond with the business and wish this for the long term.

Traces of Frontline Excellence from the Past

Providing customer service with just soft skills is temporary and superficial unless spirituality is introduced. Soft skills become a tool box without its main tool. Thus this unique association of soft skills and spirituality gives an edge over competition to allow the business to retain customers. It also brings about a healthy work–life balance, excellence, and consistency in individuals.

A link between spirituality and customer service can be traced from the past. For example, Americans at one time moved away from US automobiles to Japanese cars due to quality. At the time the difference was so profound that it started a revolution in the manufacturing industry called Kaizen, the practice of 'continuous improvement' involving all employees. The US automotive industry became leading converts to quality yet were unable to win over the hearts of Americans. At the time, Americans believed the Japanese provided superior quality products. Therefore, we learn that the ultimate judge of quality, for businesses, is the customer – irrespective of any quality movements.

According to Mark W. Johnston and Greg W. Marshall in their book *Contemporary Selling: Building Relationships, Creating Value*, 'Customers buy solutions to their problems'.

Yet businesses get entangled in what they want to sell and not what problems their products can solve. This stunts the potential of their products. Similarly, sales processes need to be more user-friendly. They should also engage customers by seeking feedback opportunities for the improvements of the businesses, products, and sales personnel. The feedback should be from internal and external customers to better create a climate for service.

An internal customer is one who is internal to the organization. Internal customers are stakeholders, employees, or shareholders, but the definition also encompasses creditors and external regulators. The external customer is someone who signs on the dotted line to pay the employer and ultimately provides the income to make paycheques possible. An external customer buys company products and services.

Diagram 4:

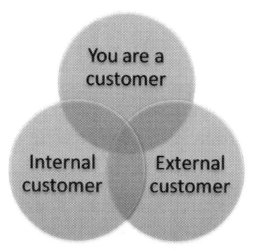

For the internal customer, 'A climate for service is the shared employee perceptions of the policies, practices and procedures, and behaviours that get rewarded and supported and are expected with regard to customer service and customer service quality,' said Benjamin Schneider, professor emeritus from the University of Maryland.

Chapter 3

Qualitative Performance

There is a difference between the terms 'customer service', 'customer experience', and 'customer experience excellence'.

Customer service is defined as the technical delivery of a product or service. This is the assistance and advice provided by a company representative for the purchase or use of a product or service. Assistance and advice can vary dependent on the kind of product or service being bought or used.

Customer experience is how a recipient feels before, during, and after the delivery of a product or service, whereas customer experience excellence is the *consistent delight* a customer feels before, during, and after the delivery of a product or service. Excellence in customer experience comes from a genuine commitment to customer service. A commitment anchored in the core of an individual makes it as genuine as can be.

Diagram 5:

Customers are comfortable with processes and experiences that are measurable and quantifiable. For example, if a restaurant commits to making a home delivery of food to a customer's home within thirty minutes, the customer expects it within that given time frame. In the meantime the customer makes arrangements related to the meal at home based on the expected timeline, which is measurable, giving the customer clarity as to what to expect. The successful experience becomes comfortable to use in the future.

A customer assumes the quality of a business and its services when factors are measurable and commitments are upheld. This gives them confidence to try new products when introduced by the business. Similarly, soft skills must be made measurable to give both the customer and business credibility. Customers express the quality of a business to others by word of mouth. This shows their loyalty to the business. To achieve this breakthrough it is vital to identify the customers' touchpoints with the company – that is, the different ways they are engaged with the company (see diagram 2). It is vital to identify the skills necessary and develop them in frontline professionals. This is a start to making lifetime experiences at each touchpoint. Companies that really want to make consistent lifetime experiences aren't going to get there by making small, incremental improvements but by boldly redefining the experiences for customers.

The best experiences are those that consistently go beyond customer expectations and with excellence within any and all interactions with the customer.

Achieving this requires trained service personnel with the right attitude. The loss of repeat business is attributed to subsequently indifferent attitudes. This indifference is born from human wounds – that is, having been hurt by various perceptions that present themselves through circumstances. This happens due to the lack of acknowledging one's own perfection, from a general framework, of individual attitude. When one is wounded in this manner recovery surely takes time. It's like scraping a knee, only in this case, abilities get scraped. Just as medicine is applied to an open wound and healing irritates the skin, the mind finally seeks truth and thus irritates abilities. As recovery from experiences take place, the mind takes on a healthy framework of individual attitude, which carries all kinds of experiences and circumstances that are fulfilling; new abilities are eventually realized. The conversion of weaknesses to strengths with a new and educated approach translates into the right attitude.

What is an indifferent attitude? It's neither feeling love nor hate, like or dislike, not pursuing choice. The worst someone can do to another is be indifferent. It evokes a perception of non-existence, that one is empty or hollow to the other and that one does not exist for the other. Indifference is worse than hatred and results in spiritual brokenness. To be spiritually broken is to live one's life in many ways in which one's intentions and actions are inconsistent; one's emotions are fragmented; and one's life is a consequence of deceit. The only way we can stop ourselves from an indifferent attitude is by realizing absolute ideas.

The most powerful balm for recovering from an indifferent attitude is individual affection, without limitations, which means loving oneself first. Recovery from an indifferent attitude is possible by accepting the circumstance and using emotional maturity to forgive the individual. One who takes this approach does not expect a return or even the recognition of existence. Instead, one accepts gradual recovery and realizes new abilities. One finally acknowledges the truth of experiences and newness for progress.

Absolute ideas are boundless, so human decisions empower an individual. Our attention to absolute ideas help us endure loss and gain abundance. Here, abundance is to value those things in life that have a sense of permanence. Having known this in an intrinsic fashion, we are motivated as individuals to overcome loss and seek newness.

Living in the internal universe is as important as living in the external one. The one who takes this journey engages in activities that draw the person to live the inner values on the outside with discernment. Discernment is to seek decisions from our conscience. Many can discern, but it seems few may act upon it. An integrated mind acts on discernment. If the conscience did not supply discernment, how would we live absolute ideas such as excellence and consistency?

We can strive towards abundance through discernment in order not to be narrow minded but being open minded without degrading the mind, spirit, and body. Absolute ideas exist even if you believe they don't.

Ideas such as consistency and excellence exist in our minds in their purest form whether we believe they do or not. By tapping into them we have the potential to express them in our external world. Our endeavour is to keep seeking them to realize their full potential.

Attitude consists of three elements: thoughts, emotions, and behaviours. These three must be synchronized to come together for any human processes. Use the positive of the three and move forward with it to positively impact the other elements and realize absolute ideas.

For example, an individual may be proficient at tasks assigned to him, yet he has shown an attitude for being quickly bored or disinterested. There is a high chance for a company to quickly lose such talent due to a lack of excitement. The fact is he would easily be bored or disinterested with any new task no matter what a company might assign him to keep his services and to influence his emotions towards the thought of loyalty for the company. In such a case the individual lacks a certain level of awareness within himself that could allow him to overcome this constant need for excitement. This need is rooted in his emotional boredom or disinterest. The awareness that is missing for him is 'Everyone is more than they feel'.

This awareness comes from spirituality (as defined above) that can be nurtured through behaviour modification. Boredom in a task can be overcome by seeking constant improvement in it. Being the best at the workplace does not mean that there is no more place for improvement. The comparison should not be with others but with oneself by seeking to constantly improve one's own performance. It focuses on the positive element of behaviour (tasks done well) and ultimately influences one's own emotions and thoughts over time to be profitable for oneself and the company. Attitude can easily be measured by linking spirituality with customer service. This measurement relies on frequency (the rate at which something occurs over a particular period of time or in a given sample), which is quantifiable.

The right attitude of an individual for the contribution to the business can be measured as follows:

- *Frequency of supportive action with resiliency* is how often the individual keeps a balance between the business's interest and the customer's interest and demonstrates the ability to bounce back from any weighty situation/setback.

- *Frequency in adequate knowledge communicated* is how often the individual demonstrates adequate information (enough to reach the success for the business's higher purpose). It's information that is directly proportionate to what the customer desires without breaching confidentialities.

- *Frequency in use of rights and opportunities within defined limits* is how often the individual makes the best business decisions. When there are any new decisions, individuals generally hesitate to apply and implement them and may not realize boundaries to new decisions.

- *Frequency in exactness* is how often the individual is precise to the point of excellence in the experiences for the customer and demonstrates business values as precisely as the company aims.

- *Frequency of being decision-oriented* is how often decisions are broken down into three parts: 1) intention, 2) action, and 3) consequence. That is, a decision is demonstrated with the right aim, the right things to do, and with the right result as calculated.

- *Frequency of fearlessness* is how often the individual demonstrates audaciousness within the limitations stipulated by policies and procedures.

- *Frequency of trustworthiness* is how often the individual demonstrates he or she can be trusted by customers.

- *Frequency in being consistent* is how the individual repeats the delivery of positive results through excellence in experiences to the customer and demonstrates he or she is sure of what is being conveyed.

- *Frequency of self-reward* is how often the individual rewards him or herself upon reaching short- and long-term goals rather than waiting for external endorsements. For example, a self-reward is achieved by good deeds for oneself, seeking good advice for oneself, giving personal time to oneself for self-development, or through buying gifts for oneself.

- *Frequency of balance in core emotions visible in situations* is how often the individual has demonstrated his or her emotions are under control and the person's work is governed by steady emotions towards a customer, their team members, and the business.

- *Frequency that the individual has discrete behaviour of isolated experiences* is how often the individual shares the best practices he or she knows with team members and the business, and how little the person withholds information that can be valuable to the progress of the business.

- *Frequency that the individual demonstrates behaviour of a holistic approach towards customers* is how often the individual has demonstrated he or she has a 360-degree awareness of business channels, processes, procedures, systems, and skills.

When frequencies gradually increase, the individual is closer to holistic progress. As individuals evolve, their professional and personal progress evolves. This is measurable.

Body Language

Body Language is the conscious and subconscious movements and postures by which attitudes are communicated.

In *The Definitive Book of Body Language*, authors Barbara Pease and Allan Pease say that to convey a consistent message to the customer, the application of body language plays a big role: it is 55 per cent of any communication and/or message.

Pioneers in body language studies include

- Charles Darwin, who was an influential academic of body language pre–twentieth century. Darwin's studies have been validated in modern studies of body language.
- Albert Merhabian, a pioneer researcher of body language in the 1950s, found that the total impact of a message is about 7 per cent verbal (words only), 38 per cent vocal (tone of voice, inflections, and other sounds), and 55 per cent non-verbal (body language).
- anthropologist Ray Birdwhistell, who initiated a study of non-verbal communication – what we call kinesics. He estimated that humans can make around two hundred fifty thousand facial expressions. He also studied that 60 to 80 per cent of business communication is attributed to body language.

There are three rules to accurately read body language:

1) *Read gestures in clusters:* Body language is an outward reflection of a person's emotional condition. Just as a single word cannot explain a sentence of several words, a single gesture cannot explain an emotional condition without it being grouped with all the other gestures. This method of combining all gestures to determine a person's emotional condition is known as 'reading gestures in clusters'.
2) *Look for congruence:* Non-verbal signals carry five times more impact than the verbal channel. So when the two are contradictory (or incongruent), people usually rely on non-verbal content to arrive at a message and disregard the verbal content. Congruence is when the verbal message matches the non-verbal message.
3) *Read gestures in context*: All gestures should be considered in the context in which they occur. So watch for things

within the environment – to name a few, the temperature within a room, tight clothes that restrict movement, and the number of people in the room. This could be attributing to the cluster of gestures.

For example, certain gestures can be viewed as defensive and reserved, yet it could be cold in the room, and the body gesture could suggest this too. Therefore, one would also observe a tight-lipped smile showing rejection, heavy-laden eyes showing disinterest, and arms folded showing reservation, but perhaps the environment isn't the cause. Something might have been said or expressed that did not allow openness, as the cluster, congruence, and context of body language all seem to suggest the same sentiment of attitude.

Fake Body Language

Body language can be misread, just as it is difficult to fake it. Body language is linked to brain function, which means faking body language is not easily possible. When we fake body language, the body has micro signals such as pupil dilation, lip twitches, and eyebrow movements, to name a few. The faked gestures do not match the verbal message. Faked body language can only be done successfully by a professional con artist.

The Power of Hands

- *Open palms* suggest honesty, truthfulness, genuineness, and openness.
- *Hidden palms* suggest concealing facts and closed to being approached.
- *Habitually open palms* encourage the tendency to be truthful by diminishing untruthfulness.

- *Palm-up position* is used as a submissive and non-threatening gesture that encourages the other to be accepting of the ideas of the person with palm-up position.
- *Palm-down position* projects immediate authority. The other will sense that an order has been given by the person with the palm-down position. The response can also be of feeling antagonized as an emotional condition, dependent on the relationship with the one responding.
- *Palm-closed finger-pointed position* suggests the finger-pointer is beating the other person into submission, which evokes negative feelings in most listeners, as this gesture is symbolic of a club clutched in hand. This is a negative and annoying gesture.
- *Habitual finger-pointers* are viewed as rude and aggressive and can try practicing the palm-up or palm-down position to create a more relaxed atmosphere and have a more positive effect on others.
- *Squeezing fingertip on thumb position* suggests a gesture to say 'OK'. This gesture is taught to politicians, speakers, businesspeople, and leaders. This gesture is received as being thoughtful, goal –oriented, and focused.
- *Holding hands,* when one has a hand over the other's and is a few steps ahead, suggests that the person ahead can be the decision maker in the relationship, while the person behind (with the hand underneath) is possibly submissive towards this dominant partner.

Forms of Greeting

Shaking hands is a custom from our ancient past. It evolved as a way people could cement a deal with each other. Shaking hands is the interlocking and shaking of palms. American and European countries adopt handshakes on initial greeting and on departure in all business contexts and increasingly at social events attended by women and men.

However, not all cultures use handshakes to greet each other. Here are a few modern cultural examples of greetings other than handshake.

Japan: Bowing from the waist upwards is the traditional greeting.

Thailand: Wai is an opposite palms contact gesture that looks similar to praying.

Germany: Germans heartily pump a handshake two or three times, sometimes including an additional hold time of an extra two pumps.

Muslim countries (for greeting women): A head nod is traditional. Arabic men traditionally kiss each cheek. However, the handshake is accepted in modern business communications between men.

Asia and Africa: 'Namaste' is the traditional greeting in India. However, a limp-gripped handshake is acceptable in both India and Africa.

Women and Handshakes

Across cultures, women who initiate a handshake are rated in most places as more open-minded and therefore make better first impressions.

When meeting a woman customer for the first time, a smile and nod is a traditional custom unless the customer extends her hand to shake first, the reason being that a handshake offered in such a circumstance can produce negative results (such as a feeling of being forced). A handshake is acceptable if an earlier relationship has been established. A handshake is an acceptable gesture when closing a deal. It is a seal of agreement as mentioned earlier.

The Three Basic Perceptions of a Handshake

Dominance is transmitted by turning your palm face down above the receiver's palm in the handshake. Your palm does not have to face directly down but is the upper hand and communicates that you want to take control of the encounter. The receiver of your handshake says, 'He's trying to dominate me; I'd better be cautious.'

Submission: The opposite of a dominant handshake is to offer your hand with your palm facing upwards – symbolically giving the other person the upper hand. The receiver says, 'I can dominate this person. He'll do what I want.'

A submissive handshake can be effective if you want to give the other person control or allow him to feel that he is in charge of the situation, such as in the case of making an apology to whom your handshake is submissive to.

For another person using a submissive handshake with you, see the cluster of gestures following the handshake for an accurate reading of whether the person is indeed submissive. Women tend to give a soft handshake to imply submissiveness. In a business context this approach can be disastrous for a woman because men then may give attention to her feminine qualities and not take her seriously. This does not mean women in business need to act in a masculine way; they simply can avoid signals of a feminine kind, such as soft handshakes, short skirts, and towering heels, if they want equal status.

Equality: When two dominant people shake hands, a symbolic power struggle takes place. Each tries to turn the others' palm into a submissive position. The result is both palms remain in a vertical position, and this creates a feeling of equality and mutual respect because neither is prepared to give in. The receiver says, 'I feel comfortable with this person.'

A good rapport is created when

1) palms are in the vertical position so that no one is dominant or submissive; and
2) you apply the same pressure in your handshake as you receive.

The average male hand can exert twice the power of a female hand, so allowance must be made when shaking hands with women. Remember that the handshake was evolved as a gesture to say hello or good-bye or to seal an agreement. The handshake must be always warm, friendly, and positive.

How to Manage Power Play

There are two techniques to disarm someone who consistently gives you a dominant handshake by using the following steps. They switch the power from him to you.

A. **Step-to-the-Right Technique**

Step forward with your left foot as you reach to shake hands.

Move your right foot forward into the other person's personal space.

Bring your left leg near your right and then shake hands.

B. **The-Hand-on-Top Technique**

Respond with the palm-up position of your right hand.

Put your left hand over his right to form a double-handed grip.

Straighten the handshake.

If a person is purposely trying to intimidate the individual, grasp his hand on top and shake it.

The Power of Smiles

The first recorded scientific studies into smiling were done in the early part of the nineteenth century when French scientist Guillemet Duchenne de Boulogne used electro-diagnostic and electrical stimulation to distinguish between the smile of real enjoyment and other kinds of smiles. He discovered that smiles are controlled by two sets of muscles:

- the zygomaticus major muscle runs down the side of the face and connects to the corner of the mouth. This muscle pulls back the mouth to show the teeth and enlarges the cheeks. This muscle can be consciously controlled.
- the orbicularis oculi muscle pulls the eyes back, and this makes the eyes narrow. This muscle acts independently and reveals the true feelings of a genuine smile. So the first place to check the sincerity of a smile is to look for wrinkle lines beside the eyes. Genuine smiles are generated by the unconscious brain and is hence automatic.

In a genuine smile

- the mouth muscles move;
- cheeks raise;
- eyes crease up; and
- eyebrows dip.

Smiling is a submission signal. Babies cry at birth, begin smiling at five weeks, and laugh between their fourth and fifth months. When the zygomaticus is pulled horizontally or downwards and the orbicularis oculi doesn't move, those people are considered anxious or fearful, smiling a nervous smile.

A smile shows another person that you are non-threatening and asks to be accepted at a personal level. An apology offered with a smile is more effective than an apology that does not offer a smile for minor grievances.

The Mirroring Concept

A smile often results in a smile in response. Smiles are contagious, even when the smile is fake. The mirror neuron in the brain triggers the part responsible for the recognition of faces and expressions and causes an instant mirroring reaction. People automatically copy the facial expressions they see. Regular smiling, even when you don't feel like it, is important because smiling directly influences other people's attitudes and how they respond. The more you smile the more positive the reactions others will give you. A research conducted thirty years ago, as noted by Barbara Pease and Allan Pease in their book *The Definitive Book of Body Language*, states that smiling at the beginning of a negotiation where people size each other up results in better relationships, successful outcomes, and higher sales.

Smiling is essentially a submissive signal and a disarming gesture. It has a powerful effect on the mind as the brain can separate a smile from every other part of the face upon observation. A fake smile is stronger on one side of the face. The cortex that specializes in facial expressions is in the right hemisphere of the brain, which sends signals to the left side of the body. Therefore, false facial emotions are more prominent on the left side of the face. In a genuine smile, both hemispheres instruct each side to act with symmetry.

Commonly, women need to smile less when dealing with dominant men as the smile from a woman can be misinterpreted as appeasement. Especially in business settings, a woman should mirror the amount of smiling a man does. If men want to be more persuasive with women they need to smile more in all contexts.

Five Common Types of Smiles

There is a saying that laughter is the best medicine. Laughter attracts friends, improves health, and extends life. When we laugh, every organ in the body is affected in a positive way. Laughter exercises the body and increases the amount of oxygen in the blood because our breathing quickens. This expands blood vessels close to the surface of the skin, which is why we go red on the face when we laugh. Humour has a positive impact in counteracting stress. When humans are upright in posture, they have greater freedom in producing intended sounds, good speech, and good laughter.

The older we become the more serious we become about life. An adult laughs an average of fifteen times a day, but a pre-schooler laughs an average of four hundred times a day. Yet laughing should be frequently introduced into our daily communication since research by Richard Davidson, professor of psychology and psychiatry from University of Wisconsin in Madison, showed that the left hemisphere has a surge of electrical activities that bring spontaneous happiness even with intentionally produced smiles and laughter. (Davidson derived this conclusion by hooking his subjects to electroencephalography [EEG] machines.)

Endorphins are chemicals released by the brain when we laugh. They have a similar chemical composition to morphine and heroin and have a tranquillizing effect on the body, while building the immune system.

- *The Tight-Lipped Smile:* In this smile the lips are stretched tight across the face in a straight line and the teeth are concealed. It sends the message that a secret, an opinion, or an attitude is withheld. It is most commonly a rejection signal.

- *The Drop-Jaw Smile:* In this smile the lower jaw is simply dropped to give the impression that the person is laughing or playful. It is used to encourage happy reactions in their audiences.

- *The Twisted Smile:* This smile shows opposite emotions on either side of the face. These are deliberate and show sarcasm.

- *Sideways Looking-up Smile:* Here the head is turned down and away while looking up with a tight-lipped smile; the one smiling looks juvenile, playful, and secretive. This is a coy smile that emotes parental feelings in a man (making men want to care and protect), and a favourite for men in women.
- *The George W Bush Grin:* Here there is a permanent smirk on the face which commonly gives the message that the one smiling may know something others don't.

Body language plays a big part in understanding customers and monitoring your own gestures to know attitude. Body language speaks of an individual's spiritual disposition. However, there are several aspects of spirituality tied to customer service other than body language that can make individuals promoters of a business. The promoters of a business are customers, yet the internal customer and external customer come together to promote a business by the push of 'transactional marketing' towards 'relationship marketing'.

Transactional marketing is when the relationship of a business with a customer is transient to exchange goods and services for money. Focus is on hitting targets and profits, with interest on today's sale rather than ensuring the business will always sell to the customer, certainly not pursuing lifetime experiences. Sales and marketing hold responsibilities with emphasis on order taking rather than on fulfilment and delivery.

Relationship marketing is when the relationship with a customer is long term and ensures repeat business and lifelong loyalty. The representative of the business works towards retaining relationships by allotting resources, such as integrating the entire marketing mix (people, products, processes, and physical evidence) and providing memorable experiences, to build loyalty. For a successful business, everyone is responsible for sales and marketing by providing lifetime value and retaining targeted customers. Therefore, a promoter is one who advocates the business's products and services and the company itself. The critical success factor for a business is its employees, especially those who interface with customers. Their enthusiasm about the company's products, brands, customers, etc. can be the alchemy towards providing lifetime experiences. Businesses can determine the success of their customer experience by asking one simple question to their internal and external customers: 'How likely would you recommend this business's products to a friend or colleague?'

The ultimate test for any customer relationship is whether the business grows and operates at peak efficiency and effectiveness. A few questions a business should ask employees:

'Does the business help employees clarify and simplify the job of satisfying customers?'

'Does the business help them identify and engage their best customers?'

'Does the business allow them to compare their performance from week to week and month to month?'

Businesses that achieve long-term profitable growth have commitment to excellence and consistency in customer service higher than the average businesses, thus, on average, leaders grow at a higher rate than competitors. For this to work there must be strong leadership commitment.

Chapter 4

Frontline Leadership

Transformational leadership is a style of leadership where the leader is charged with identifying the needed change, creating a vision to guide the change through inspiration, and executing the change in tandem with committed members of the group.

A leader facilitates individual growth and the growth of a business with the following links between spirituality and customer service:

- demonstrates a passion for their purpose
- practices their values consistently
- leads with their hearts as well as their heads
- establishes long-term relationships
- practices self-discipline to get results
- displays courage to do what's right (not what's easy)
- leads by example
- is consistently inspirational, motivational, and personal
- is audacious by setting direction and driving the vision
- changes mind-sets and thinks differently to move the needle
- leads by example and walks the talk
- constantly innovates, energizes, and influences self and teams
- listens, invests, and develops people as the future of a business while making the right choices
- mentors and encourages teams to deliver great things

- empowers people and gives them creative freedom
- inspires and shapes the behaviour of others

These can be achieved by staying close to one's core human qualities with the human conscience. What is here and now is a mix of both, as some are temporary and some are permanent. Why not understand and accept what we actually have? Some have material wealth, and this is not wrong, even though it is temporary, as long as we have the wisdom to place it in the right areas and as long as we have not done wrong to gain it. Similarly, material poverty is not wrong, as this poverty is also temporary. The relieving news is that wealth is not merely material gain, and the greatest wealth is when we grant truth to the self.

But there are moments that we do wrong and get so used to the consequence of the wrong that it does not *seem* wrong anymore. Tainted by superficial desires, perception forms. The conscience is difficult to tap into when we taint it with overwhelming disbeliefs and perception in the conscious mind, which the conscience originally does not recognize it as the authentic. We mend this habit of mental misdirection with the integration of our conscious mind and the acceptance of what we originally knew.

As an analogy: a diamond is transparent, brilliant, and precious. It's basically coal, a fuel, a hard mineral that can ignite. So a diamond is merely a mineral (coal) under immense pressure. Consider people as coal placed on this earth. It is up to us whether we want to be called a diamond or fuel. A diamond is integrating and consistent. Fuel is disintegrating and temporary. We have an open choice, which is to either be fuel or a diamond. Will we work well under immense pressure and allow the diamond to emerge? We are merely coal in our truest form; that is, we are simple. We need to make decisions that are integrating and consistent and not ones that are disintegrating and temporary. So we are privileged to be under immense pressure for our diamond to emerge.

If we work towards this, we will realize that we all have the same potential as that coal. We expand abilities to make ourselves capable of strength under pressure.

Perception partially takes form in our imaginations and becomes firm in egos while the truth of 'what is' presents the absolute. This inspires us to receive abundance, such as the abundance that makes known to us our human potential.

Following are seventeen human qualities that every frontline leader (or change agent) should display for the pursuit of excellence and consistency as absolute ideas, converting human potential to reality with the conscience. When spirituality is linked to customer service, the frontline leader is

1) *an innovator* who introduces new ideas, concepts, and skills. Everyone can be innovative, but those who release these new ideas, concepts and skills – are recognized. Innovators constantly reinvent themselves by seeking to improve what they were already doing. Innovators find new ways to do difficult tasks in easier ways. Customers like the best possible services in easiest possible ways.

2) *open to change:* change is constant, which is to say people change, processes change, services change, systems change, etc. Change happens all the time. One thing that is consistent in building a bold experience for customers. Employee acceptance of change is imperative, and using the opportunities of change while staying within its limitations is a necessity for being open to change.

   When a company introduces a new policy for employees, they use the policy for the rights and opportunities it presents. Further, they stay within the limitations it presents. A new policy for employees is a form of bold change. For a policy to influence employees productively, it is important for them to be open to change and to constructively exercise the policy as per the stipulated guidelines for the best possible results. Change is unchangeable in itself and a concept of evolution, so if evolution is desired in businesses for excellence, then a frontline leader demonstrates being open to change. If frontline leaders do not change along with any external changes made, then they are prone to being left behind.

3) *agile:* being flexible to change can boost the effectiveness of a leader. The measurement of a good leader is directly proportionate to how quickly a leader responds to change, which means the speed at which a transformational leader takes action defines and sets a leader apart from the rest of those who merely manage and don't exactly lead.

For example, a transformational leader decides to use the Pareto Principle (also known as the 80-20 rule), which states that for any set of events, roughly 80 per cent of the effects come from 20 per cent of the causes. So 20 per cent rests on those things that are 'urgent', which gives 80 per cent of results. What usually needs to be done at the workplace is not always urgent. This 20 per cent gives greater results if attended to quicker; hence carrying an impact of 80 per cent. This correlates with the ABC analysis shown in diagram 6.

Diagram 6:

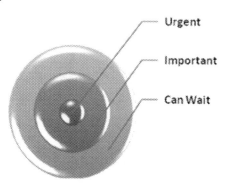

Urgent

Important

Can Wait

4) *an investor:* transformational leaders must constantly update themselves with the current best practices without being asked to do so. They choose to invest in their education and training to take their career to the next level. Such investment will bring ideas and inspiration. Motivation comes from outside oneself, and inspiration comes from inside oneself. An employee who is inspired believes in himself as a catalyst of change. The transformational leader becomes more than an asset to the business; he or she becomes a brand ambassador. This kind of leader may even invest in the stocks and shares of a business as a stakeholder. Investment in oneself redefines a leader and promotes his or her economic status.

5) *inclined to personalize:* a transformational leader strikes a balance between the customer and the business; the leader personalizes this responsibility to the customer and strives to achieve continued relationships. This leader knows the customers inside-out: their likes, their dislikes, and so on. It is suggested to identify the personality types of the customers and to use adaptive behaviours with them.

6) *a collaborator:* a transformational leader recognizes that collaboration is the only way forward to achieve success. It is all about teamwork. A leader involves others to succeed by sharing his knowledge, skills, and abilities while open to the ideas of others.

7) *audacious:* a leader is fearless, enterprising, dynamic, and spirited. This leader is a risk-taker who thinks uniquely, unafraid to express the self and to bring out employee and customer feedback, converting all transactions into win-win situations.

8) *action-oriented:* the new leader is not only a *dreamer* but a *doer.* A leader must have both attributes to demonstrate his

or her ability to realize dreams. He or she takes personal responsibility and ownership to move from incremental changes to quantum leaps.

9) *results driven:* a new leader has the make-it-happen skill set. This leader is not satisfied until having achieved desired results.

10) *humble:* people usually have the perception that humility exhibits under-confidence. Humility can also be perceived as the highest level of confidence derived from achievements because achievements constantly remind transformational leaders that they do not 'know it all' while they develop and grow. In this perception of humility, transformational leaders are dignified and ready to face their weaknesses to convert into strengths, thus not being afraid to talk about their weaknesses. The transformational leaders' actions and achievements speak for themselves and do not require a forced spotlight. Those who are haughty are meagre in ambition and fail to visualize continuity in self-progress.

11) *decision-oriented:* the new leader breaks a decision into three parts: intention, action, and consequence.

Before I explain the three parts, it is essential to understand some terms:

Idea is a thought for a possible course of action.

Intention is an aim towards a possible course of action.

Action is the process of doing something to achieve an aim.

Consequence is an important result or effect of an action.

Decision is a conclusion or resolution reached after consideration.

Fidelity is the degree of exactness with which something is copied or reproduced.

Favourability is the degree of advantage to a decision.

Qualify decisions by questioning.

1. Is the intention towards the decision sound?
2. Does the action support the intention?
3. Can the estimated consequence of the action be expected with high probability?
4. Are the intentions, actions, and consequences favourable to the decision?
   If the answer is yes to all four questions, then take the decision and question the results.
5. Is the estimated consequence the same as or similar to the actual consequence?
6. Does the intention, action, and consequence show fidelity to the decision?

12) *self-rewarding:* rewards are not just monetary, such as salaries, bonuses, increments, cash rewards, etc. Even though they endorse performance, promote progress, and strive to produce growth professionally and personally, these don't bring out the best in an individual. It is important to reward oneself. These rewards can play the part of inspiration for oneself. The following are ways to endorse the self and promote progress by one's own resources:

o   Propel self to act out. For example, an employee has a set of key performance indicators (KPIs). These are the duties a person is expected to perform. KPIs are the first type of work to attend to, ensuring that the role produces the due expected by an employee. However, after KPIs are met, an employee is often given a choice of working 'outside the box' –that is, attending to those work-related duties that can enhance an employee's learning; display increased productivity for a business; save time for the profitability in business results; and many other advantages for the business. This gives an edge to the business. By this, a business gains but the employee gains as well by expanding their horizons for professional and personal progress, which is a reward in itself for their own future.

o Consistent best practices should follow with giving self the desirable yet infrequent personal choices. For example, employees' best practices are the things they do that gives the business maximum benefit. These best practices should be consistent and not sporadic, and when consistently executed, should be rewarded by oneself with personal choices (deeds, gifts, time, etc.).

o Set short- and long term goals. The achievement of these are rewards in themselves and convert weaknesses to strengths. For example, an employee sets a weekly target to achieve leading to a cumulative achievement of monthly, quarterly, half yearly, and annual targets. An employee's target need not be what has been stipulated by the company but can be something greater than it and reasonably achievable. The human disposition in the achievements of these personal goals are rewards in itself while a business constantly redefines their expectations from an employee, thus putting an employee on a *sort of* fast track for lateral and/or hierarchical growth.

13) *a challenger of self:* the new leader always challenges the old way of doing things. He or she encourages others to think and devise new ways of doing things. Challenging the self is a positive and realistic movement forward from being locked into ancient practices and as a provider of solutions to society.

14) *a listener:* a leader is not absorbed in the clutter of his or her mind but seeks constant feedback from the customers and frontline teams. The leader seriously considers their views for implementation.

15) *responsive:* the new leader responds with a thought-through interaction; this leader knows the difference between reacting and responding. (A reaction is from impulse, whereas response is a considered action coming sometimes through instinct and mostly thought through before execution.)

16) *a deliverer:* a transformational leader not only makes the right decisions and pursues the right action with positive results but does so in a consistent manner to boost relationships and increase long-term profitability.

17) *a communicator:* a transformational leader speaks in a clear and practical manner while articulating the direction the team is heading. The desired end result should also be vividly communicated, and employees should be given feedback as to where they stand in relation to the desired goals. The leader eliminates miscommunication and misunderstanding. Employees need motivation to perform at their best, as much as inspiration, since motivation comes from the external world and inspiration comes from within. Gain the agreement and commitment necessary to elevate the business vision by understanding employees' likes and dislikes and their motivations (e.g., recognizing and applauding their accomplishments, providing training to increase their knowledge base, and establishing a pleasant work environment to perform at their highest level). Determination means having the tenacity to finish the race regardless of the hurdles that come your way. Depend on yourself and your teams' courage, stamina, strength, and perseverance to realize the business vision. By displaying this

endurance, transformational leaders show employees that hard work and smart work pays off in the end.

Transformational leaders know how to assemble the appropriate team to get the job done. This includes enlisting, empowering and equipping qualified team leaders and other willing individuals who do not have leadership roles. The transformational leader understands the importance of assigning tasks based on individual characteristics and abilities. Leaders are infinite students with the introspective ability to keep learning about the self, alone or with the assistance of others to maintain a flourishing bond with employees with the nurture and support of relationships. This means looking outside the self, concentrating on what's best for the team, and transferring this energy to employees so they emulate this behaviour, as well as being true to integrating spirituality and customer service. Provide employees with the proper learning tools to elevate the vision to its greatest height.

Specifically, workers need stimulating work that challenges and expands their minds and facilitates the desire to keep learning. As the transformational leader, recognize this and work towards improving employee intellectuality. As change in a business environment is inevitable, courageously recognize the need for change and initiate it accordingly (for example, learning and adapting to an upgraded accounting system, or adjusting to an employee who has just been promoted to management). The transformational leader effectively shows employees why the change is needed, how it will benefit them and the business, and how to embrace it.

Eventually, whatever or whoever may be at the centre of our focus will be our driving force. In common terms, if the centre of our focus is not, and other than the seat of our conscience, then

- human affection is human sacrifice/surrender (a compromise),
- any law is human sensibility (where comfortable, applicable),

- self-liberation is human satisfaction (a temporary reward),
- life is human survival (the struggle to even exist),
- loyalty is human safety (to guard oneself from being harmed),
- light to the human mind is human saturation (that when temporary things seems enough human beings 'may' turn to spirituality), and
- longevity is human sophistication (the assertion that the temporary lived in excess is OK).

This is frustrated intelligence brought about by misdirection.

No one knows how anyone else feels or thinks in any given moment. The only feelings and thoughts a person fully knows is his or her own.

Human brilliance is drawn by the acknowledgment of the wrongs in our lives and the correction of them. The greatest wrongs human beings live are drawn from the human mind.

By this I mean we are merely simple in our truest form and make life far too complicated, resulting in tainted perceptions. The greatest results are drawn from the truth. This truth is useful when brought to the human being to attain clarity of how things are.

Spirituality is the only way the person we are can be fully known. The fullness of the person we are is our human potential, which directly coincides with performance in customer service.

The search, discovery, realization, acceptance, humility, truth known, human brilliance, and relationship between perfection and the human person will be the beginnings of the spiritual age.

Chapter 5

Professionalism

Professionalism can be defined as the skill, good judgment, and polite behaviour that is expected from a person who is trained to do a job well. Professionalism must display the following attributes in frontline professionals.

Strongly Reflect the Customer's Identity

Know your customer. Seek information about the customer, such as customer's likes, dislikes, interests, and disinterests. Further, know the customer's family status and working capacities. Methods of extracting this information is different from business to business. After this information is acquired, a professional personalizes any experience with a business with this information, making an interaction valid and intrinsically identifiable for the customer.

Satisfy Company Higher Objectives

The objective of a frontline salesperson is taking the interaction from just a transacted sale to a memorable experience. The ultimate objective is to retain the customer for repeat business. Every business wishes to retain customers. As a frontline professional, it is your duty to make an optimal effort to convert all customers to advocates and retain them. Such customers should be targeted and converted to advocates. Advocates become brand champions. Work towards this with every customer as a frontline professional and retain those customers who can become brand champions.

Leave Nothing to Chance

There is a potential for every customer to become a brand champion. Be patient and address any doubts regarding customers. Address all customer enquiries and accomplish the possibility of the customer becoming a brand champion.

Set and Meet Expectations

Customers are often undecided when it comes to purchases until some information or doubts are clarified and eliminated. Don't only be an 'order taker'. Address the customer's expectations with realistic results. Convert each transaction into a win-win situation. A customer benefits owning a product or a relationship with the business through a service. The business benefits by acquiring a new customer. The frontline professional benefits by meeting his daily sales and service target with a customer who is likely to return repeat business. This is excellence in service. By meeting customers' expectations consistently the frontline professional has delivered excellence.

Be Effortless

Every interaction will become effortless through practice. This makes you a professional. This encourages a better relationship with the customer. The more strained you appear, the more strained the customer will feel.

Be Stress Free

Keep customers stress-free by being stress-free yourself. Project a pleasing disposition. Show passion and enthusiasm by enjoying your work. Since work tasks are routine, your attitude can make them enjoyable. Remember: a customer can sense your passion and enjoyment and responds equally.

Indulge in the Senses

There are five basic senses. When you are stress-free your senses are heightened towards the delivery of excellence. Engaging a customer with these senses will lead to excellent customer experiences. For example, bring notice to a fresh smell of a perfume, a soft touch of a fabric, a good tune of a song, a beautiful colour of the product, or a tangy taste to a dish on the menu.

Be Socially Engaging

Being sociable is an enduring quality towards being a frontline professional. Whoever you meet becomes an opportunity to develop a long-term relationship for your company. Keep discrete behaviour for time to engage with people. For example, a salesperson of an automotive company received many referrals from those customers whom he understood and were pleased with his actions. Those customers he was unable to adapt his behaviour to became transactional customers for a one-time-purchase. Products don't sell themselves anymore, because competition has a vast array of the same product. What gives a business an edge over competition are frontline staff who develop long-term relationships with customers by displaying excellence and consistency in what they do.

Put the Customer in Control

This does not mean you're not in control of a situation; this means you lead your customer from the back rather than the front. That is, allow customers to express themselves more in any interaction, steer the conversation by listening well, and lead the conversation by asking questions. It is by listening that you will know what solutions to provide.

Consider the Emotions

Customers are emotional about their purchases, especially those higher-cost purchases. For example, the purchase of a car or house can be an emotional experience, especially when there is a mortgage that ties a customer to financial debt for years. A car or house is an asset to the customer yet a liability to fund the mortgage regularly. These costs seem inconsequential to customers when they are appreciated, listened to, and felt cared for.

Chapter 6

Integration of Sales and Service

For the frontline personnel who are directly in communication with the external customer, certain techniques can be adopted to best implement the approach of going beyond frontline excellence. *The approach is packaged in the following steps as technique. These are not rehearsed responses. Instead, they are ways to develop your response.*

The following approach is commonly attributed to American advertising and sales pioneer E. St. Elmo Lewis. I expound on it for integrating customer service and sales.

Fact Finding

You gain the *attention* of the customer by asking open-ended questions beginning with what, where, why, when, who, and how. This helps determine the customer's needs so as to pitch the right product. For example, in the financial services industry, a few questions a consultant could ask of a prospect while planning his investments are

- What is your name?
- How many members are in your family?
- What is your age?
- When do you plan to retire?
- What are your short- and long-term financial goals?

- What investments have you made so far, and have these worked well for you?
- What do you hope to achieve with your newly desired investment?
- Why do you desire premium investments over a lump-sum investment?
- When and how do you see yourself using the potential moneys from the investment?
- Who would you like to make as the nominee?
- How would you like to contribute to the investment?

This could even start with a cold call, the marketing process of approaching prospective customers, typically via telephone, email, or social network, who were not expecting such an interaction. The word 'cold' is used because the person receiving the call is not expecting it or has not specifically asked to be contacted by a salesperson. A cold call is usually the start of a sales process generally known as telemarketing.

You could have simply acquired names and phone numbers from a database or reference with no further information. Such prospective customers are many in the market and could be potential clients. Handling them can be a challenge. Here are a few steps to make successful cold calls.

The WIN Formula

People who have money must have a good reason or need to part with it for any goods and/or services. There is an art to getting them to open up so you can qualify them. By 'qualify' I mean asking those questions that will give you the relevant information about them and their need. Any prospective customers must have the following conditions. This technique is called the WIN formula:

Will: Prospective customers must have the desire to meet and to close business.

Income: Prospective customers must have disposable income for purchase.

Need: Prospective customers must have a need or desire for the product or service.

The most important aspect for a successful cold call is for you to be in the right frame of mind when you place a call. If you are in a negative mood, you will project this on the phone, and the customer will respond accordingly. Remember that in cold calls, your first impression is your lasting impression!

To create a positive frame of mind, the following could be done:

As per telemarketing standards, take a ten minute break after every two hours of being on the phone. This line of work is of high stress, and there is no room for mistakes. The telemarketer must refresh his or her mind every two hours.

Since we are all human and not perfect, the break helps us loosen up and come back refreshed until the next break. This is healthy. In those ten minutes, occupy your time with something that refreshes you, such as music, deep breaths, a short walk outside, a glass of water, or reading. Do what suits you best!

Your frame of mind on a call could be directly proportionate to the frame of mind of the prospective customer. So if a prospective customer is speaking in a loud voice, so might you, and if a prospective customer quiets down, then so could you. Mirror a prospective customer as much as possible in this regard, as this is one way to gain his or her attention. Always be pleasant with a gentle smile on your face as a smile can be 'heard' in your voice by the person at the receiving end. This is part of the professionalism that you would seek if you were to call.

When a positive frame of mind is created to bring out your best, you can expect the best to materialize soon enough.

Use of Voice

Q: What is tone of voice?

A: The quality of a person's voice (be cordial and inviting)

Q: What is voice modulation?

A: A change in stress, pitch, loudness (be clear and harmonious)

Q: What is Intonation?

A: The use of changing pitch to convey syntactic information (to be paced or mirrored)

Q: What is Syntax?

A: The arrangement of words and phrases to create well-formed sentences in a language (to be fluent)

A cold call is like a broadcast or a performer on stage or a teacher in a classroom where you have to engage the audience to make them listen. Performers engage the audience with their skills because they can be visualized. Broadcasters engage the listeners with their voice augmented, perhaps with other sounds like pouring water into a glass, or footsteps, or a knock on the door, etc., as done in radio plays.

Any message, whether visual or audio, sends subliminal commands to the prospective listeners. Telemarketers engage their customers by modulating their voices and asking the right questions. Avoid speaking in a monotone. Try to speak with a gentle movement of your voice, from a slightly high pitch towards a slightly low pitch and vice versa (maintaining your gentle smile and mirrored volume of voice, as mentioned earlier).

A telemarketer modulates his or her voice to make a prospective customer comfortable and engaged. When a prospective customer is comfortable, he or she will listen to the telemarketer with intent. There is a fine line between being overly familiar and being professional with the use of voice modulation. If you are out to directly command the prospective customer with an aggressive tone, don't be surprised by his or her resistance. If you are out to moan with your voice, remember that no one wants to hear sorrowful litanies … and so on.

So be professional and natural with the way you use your larynx for a cold call, and keep the prospective customer interested and alert. The speed at which you talk should usually be moderate, and once the speed in which a prospective customer speaks is identified, this pattern could be mirrored by you.

How to Listen

When you're on a call, always have a pen and pad in front of you so you can scribble notes while the prospective customer speaks. You could resort to shorthand or form short words while scribbling everything you hear, including the constant sneeze of a prospective customer to enquire on his or her cold in a follow-up call. Prospective customers like to feel cared for!

Follow some key words of your prospective customers such as, 'I may …', 'I will …', 'I should …' and note these down to identify the depth of their need and readiness to purchase.

Do not interrupt a prospective customer when he or she speaks. Listen carefully using appropriate words and sounds that you are listening. Remember that with a cold call, you should always be in control of the conversation yet let them believe they are in control. Listening does this well.

To listen well is to take an interest in your call, so that would mean being sensitive to the surroundings of the prospective customer. Try to pick up any sounds behind his or her voice to understand the surroundings and the person's natural comfort level. As an example, if you hear people talking behind your prospective customer's voice and it sounds like an official meeting, it is likely he or she will not be on the line for very long. You can ask the prospective customer to schedule a call back at his or her convenient time.

Be aware that the prospective customer may also be listening to your own surrounding sounds. Try to reduce such distractions before the call.

The Seven Basic Steps in a Cold Call

1) Greet the person and ask for a name.
2) Introduce yourself and ask for a few minutes of their time.
3) State your purpose and introduce your company.
4) Engage in a conversation and ask the right questions to qualify
5) Thank him or her for sharing information and state why you asked.
6) Identify and/or create the need to schedule a meeting.
7) Book the meeting with a technique to close (a few techniques to close are noted later in this chapter).

A successful cold call will not take longer than twenty minutes inclusive of all seven steps.

Using a Script

A script is a pre-written narration of what you will say on a cold call. The script should be to the point. It's a basic outline of what needs to be communicated.

1) It is always better to write your own script than to read off one that belongs to someone else because

- You will create a script in your own style, just like conducting a professional conversation. This helps in maintaining the consistency of your language when managing objections, which is done off-script. The conversational styles will not be different keeping it natural.

- You will know how to modulate your voice with the words you choose.

- You will be comfortable engaging in interrupted conversation with the prospective customer without the fear of trying to remember where you left off in the script when the interruption happened.

2) Familiarize yourself with the nature of your business, your target market, and the technical terms that you would require to use in your presentation. Ask a lot of questions from the one who instructs you, as your questions may just be what a prospective customer could ask.

3) Plan a script that is clear to read. Have it in front of you always, no matter how many times you have read it before. This is because even if you know the script by memory, there may come a moment that could distract you from what you were saying. Use the script to bring you back on track

Tips to Ensure a Successful Cold Call

There are three major reasons a prospect will refuse to meet:

No money – the prospective customer does not see value in the product

No need – the prospective customer does not have a need for the product

No time – the prospective customer does not have any urgency for the product

Remember: Do not sell products, sell a qualified meeting. A qualified meeting is where you establish or create a need, establish or create the urgency for the purchase, and establish or create benefits that are personalized to the prospective customers so they see value in the product. Understand who your target market is and book those prospective customers that meet this target market. For example, in financial services, qualifying a meeting should be when engaged in a conversation.

In the case regarding individuals, a financial services telemarketer could ask

- if the prospective customer is employed or has a business of his or her own.
- what the name of the company is and the customer's title in the company
- if they are married
- if they have children and how old the children are
- at what age they would like to retire
- if the prospective customer has financially planned for his or her family and what these plans are
- what their approximate monthly earnings are
- after all their expenses in a month, what are they left behind with and for how long have they been in that position

In the case regarding businesses, a financial services telemarketer could ask

- when the company was established;
- which industry and sector the company is in;
- what is their staff strength and how many directors they have;

- who is the decision maker and advisor in the company for corporate financial services;
- what the company plans and targets for the given year are.

By obtaining this information you are better prepared to identify and/or create a need for financial services. This information should be disclosed to the certified individual attending the meeting so he or she is prepared and knows what to expect.

In the course of asking these questions you could raise awareness of where the prospective customer can plan or has not planned financially to have a well-balanced and diversified financial portfolio. But you can only do this if the prospective customer is keen to listen. By doing this you make a prospective customer think to himself or herself of what could be done better.

To be able to give advice, a telemarketer needs to be certified to talk about financial subjects; hence I refer to the details of raising awareness as 'soft knowledge'.

Let the advisers conduct their role by giving the right advice and you conduct your role by a fact-find exercise to establish the target market, to analyze and establish the gap in 'need', and to book a meeting once the prospective customer has been qualified via the WIN (will, income, need) formula.

By knowing these, as a telemarketer, you will be able to use the appropriate information to manage objections. Be discrete and see what can be used to manage objections best and move to a close.

For example: in the financial services industry:

If the excuse is 'no money':

Suggest that if matters are tough now, how will they be five or ten years from now? Therefore, you suggest a meeting to plan now and safeguard the future.

He or she probably has not planned his or her wealth properly in the past and hence has no money now. Suggest a meeting to plan now and safeguard the future.

He or she has no discipline to save, and this is why you suggest a meeting – so he or she is made disciplined by setting aside a sum to safeguard the future.

He or she is probably stretched, so you suggest a meeting to review what assets to safeguard the future and give the prospective client something to spend now.

If the prospective customers have no money and if anything were to happen to them, how would their families and children survive? On what income? Therefore, you suggest a meeting to safeguard them and their family from reckless expenditure.

If the excuse is 'no need':

There is never a case where a prospect has no need. This would only mean you have to identify a need and alert it to the prospect. In certain cases a telemarketer may create the need by painting a picture of financial desire.

For example, prospects would need an income at the time of retirement; they would need funds to educate their children for higher studies; prospects would plan their own home to live in and still have enough to spend on a holiday home if need arises; most importantly, prospects would need to invest and see their money grow. Money is the means to achieve these goals and dreams, and if the prospect plans his or her money well, then there will always be funds to fulfil a need as well as future dreams.

If the prospect already has someone to look after his or her financial plans, then there is no harm in a second opinion or getting new ideas and to confirm whether he or she is being looked after well enough by current financial advisors.

If the excuse is 'no time':

If the prospect has no time, he or she is not aware of the urgency, and it is the role of the telemarketer to make the prospect aware of this. Urgency is felt when a desire is strong, and this is when the need is important. So it would help to question how important it is for the prospect to plan for a dream holiday home, retirement, and the education of his or her children. Further, makes the prospect aware that the earlier he or she plans, the better it is on their pockets because there will be more time to eliminate debts to realize his or her dreams.

Remember: a financial services telemarketer does not sell a product or service but a qualified meeting.

Identify Personality

Where the customer actively expresses *interest* in the product, identify the buying criteria of the customer and adapt your behaviour to a sale. Leave nothing to chance, and do not assume information; instead, ask to clarify any doubts.

Personality Types of Customers

As retailers we deal with many customers of different personality types on a daily basis. Of course each customer is unique. However, according to Brian Tracy in *The Psychology of Selling: Increase Your Sales Faster and Easier Than You Ever Thought Possible*, there are four basic personality types in the retail environment.

The *director*: as the name implies, these personality types have demands. They are take-charge types who know what they want and when they want it – and they want it now! They can sometimes be intimidating because they are knowledgeable, having done research or have experience with the subject. Directors are generally not into small talk; they want the facts in order to make a decision as quickly as possible. If you try to get in the way of their goal, they will plough through you and, as the expression goes, 'take no prisoners'. They don't care about anyone's interest other than their own. Their goals are very clear. They want the best possible product at the lowest possible price delivered when they want it – which is usually immediately.

How to deal with a director: Eliminate as much small talk as possible, lay out the facts, give your reasons why they should purchase something, and make it brief and to the point. Generally these personality types have high self-esteem, almost to the point of being obnoxious. One of the most valuable tools you can use here is a compliment about their direct style and decisiveness. The one thing you would avoid is to tell this personality type he or she is wrong or isn't listening to you. You must let this person make a decision. You can try to make suggestions, but make sure they are short and to the point. Remember: the director gets turned off when you present yourself in any way as a roadblock to his or her goal. Never confront the directors – stay out of their way!

The *analyzer*: analyzers usually have professions that require accuracy and analysis. These would include jobs such as accountants, engineers, or scientists, whereby they conduct research and analyze all the possibilities before making a decision. What motivates this type of personality when they come into a retail store are facts, details, product descriptions, consumer reports, product specifications, etc. They want data. Analyzers read manuals, directions, and the fine print. Like the director type, they are unimpressed by small talk and niceties when they walk into a store.

How to deal with an analyzer: Give them facts and data. Do not make a statement unless you can back it up with pertinent statistics. If the product has detailed product information and specifications manuals, give them to the analyzer. There is one major advantage when it comes to dealing with analyzers. They have done their homework. In many cases they will actually know more than a salesperson or owner, which makes them a valuable source of information. Don't be afraid to ask why they came into your store, because there *is* a reason. Their biggest asset is the knowledge of the product on sale. They have the information neatly filed away in their iPad or Smartphone to immediately refer to. *Remember: asking the analyzer's opinion is considered a silent compliment.*

The *relater* has a strong need to belong to a group. I recommend the 'my' test on this personality type. When a customer refers to 'my accountant', 'my doctor', 'my garage', 'my electrician', 'my lawyer', or 'my store', your store becomes part of his or her network. These people are usually three calls away from getting any information from a friend. They always know someone who knows someone who knows someone and so forth – the classic example of 'six degrees of separation'.

How to deal with a relater: The reason we refer to the relater shopper as a 'belonging type' is because they take an ownership position in everything they do. The easiest way to sell to this personality type is to simply ask them, 'What is your opinion of this product, and do you think we should carry it?' Their response might be something like, 'I think it looks good, and I think you should carry it. I might like something like that. Let me see it.' The bottom line is to include them in any way you possibly can, because they want to feel part of the decision-making process.

A word of caution: the relater will likely come into the store when the owner is not there and report back to the owner if someone isn't doing his or her job. On the plus side, they are wonderful customers and are a sensational source of never-ending referrals. *Remember: Inclusion is the name of the game with the relater customer.*

The *socializer*: socializers are exactly as the name implies. They are outgoing, love to talk, and love to make new friends. The socializer wants to build a relationship with people who work in the store. This personality type places likeability as one of the most important buying criteria. If they don't like you they are not going to do business with you. Socializers want to build friendships. If you talk to them like an analytical, with facts and figures, they will shut right down.

As similar as they might be to the relater, loyalty isn't as important to the socializer. If they can develop friendships in several different stores, they will go to several different stores. Socializers love to receive and give compliments. However, they tend to be self-centred. They want to go to a store where they are made to feel important. This is the one group that salespeople relate to the most because the majority of salesperson are sociable when hired.

How to deal with a socializer: The most important thing to remember is that it's not all about the merchandise; it is about the relationship. Always remember that the first thing you are selling is yourself. You can be giving merchandise away, but the socializer won't care if they don't like you. Use compliments liberally. Do whatever you have to do to remember the names of these people. Don't lose sight of the fact that although they enjoy a shopping experience and look upon it as a social event, your goal is still to sell them merchandise. Remember to keep the socializer focused, yet be light enough to make their shopping experience fun and entertaining.

The next time someone walks into your store, size them up and put them into one of these four personality categories (it's a lot easier than you think once you get the hang of it). You will then be better prepared to interact with each customer on a higher level and drastically increase your sales.

Needs Analysis

Where the customer passively expresses *desire* towards a product, service, and relationship with the company/ brand, relate the desire to the fact finding phase (see the beginning of chapter 6). Convert the desire into a need. Build and/or create needs by painting a picture for the customer to visualize backed by information. *Move from being an order taker to need fulfilment.* Personalize this experience to gain maximum responses.

Build Awareness

When the customer actively expresses a *conviction to try* the offer, explain the products with solutions to customer problems and where needs can be met, not what you would like to sell for a profit since this can lead to customer becoming a shopper and not a loyal client. Describe opportunities relevant to the customer and the benefits that the customer will derive.

Close the Deal

When the customer actively negotiates for a better price or proceeds to *purchase* the offer, identify the customer's frame of mind through a trial close. Imagine the sales presentation addressing opportunities and benefits from the phase the customer might be stuck in (i.e., attention, interest, desire, conviction, or purchase). Use multiple closing techniques mentioned in the next section below, techniques to close. Close when the prospect is in the conviction phase of the mental buying process.

Wait for the customer's buying signal: anything a prospect says or does to indicate he is ready to buy, like

o   asking more questions;
o   asking another person's opinion;

o   relaxing and becoming friendly; and

o   carefully examining the product

Remember: the first no from the prospect isn't necessarily an absolute refusal to buy.

Techniques to Close

Referring to the writings of such classics as *Marketing Communications; The Art and Science of Resort Sales; The Psychology of Persuasion: How to Persuade Others to Your Way of Thinking,* and *Success Secrets of the Online Marketing Superstars,*[1] I have culled the following terms.

Alternative close: also called the positive choice close, in which the salesperson presents the prospect with two choices, both ending in a sale.

Apology close: in which the salesperson apologizes for not yet closing the sale.

Assumptive close: in which the salesperson intentionally assumes that the prospect has already agreed to buy, and wraps up the sale.

Balance Sheet Close: in which the salesperson and the customer build together a pros-and-cons list of whether to buy the product – with a longer list of pros.

Cradle to Grave Close: in which the salesperson politely counters a customer's objections when a customer says, 'It is too soon to buy!'

---

1   Koekemoer, L and S Bird (2004). *Marketing Communications.* Lansdowne, South Africa: Juta Academic;
McCann, Dennis G and Ben Gay III (1989). *The Art and Science of Resort Sales.* Union, NJ: Hampton House;
Hogan, Kevin (1996). *The Psychology of Persuasion: How to Persuade Others to Your Way of Thinking.* Gretna, LA: Pelican Publishing;
Meyerson, Mitch (2005). *Success Secrets of the Online Marketing Superstars.* Ft Lauderdale, FL: Kaplan Business.

by telling him, 'There is never a convenient time in life to make a major purchase. This could be the best time.'

Direct Close: in which the salesperson simply and directly asks the customer to buy. Salespeople are discouraged from using this technique unless they are very sure the prospect is ready to commit.

Indirect Close: also known as the question close, in which the salesperson moves to the close with an indirect or soft question.

Minor Point Close: in which the salesperson deliberately gains agreement with the customer on a minor point, and uses it to assume the sale is closed.

Negative Assumption Close: in which the salesperson asks two final questions, repeating them until he or she achieves the sale. 'Do you have any more questions for me?' and 'Do you see any reason why you wouldn't buy this product?'

Possibility of Loss Close: also known as the pressure close, in which the salesperson points out that failing to close could result in missed opportunity.

Puppy Dog Close: in which the salesperson gives the product to the prospect on a trial basis, to test before a sale is agreed upon.

Sales Contest Close: in which the salesperson offers the prospect a special incentive to close, disarming suspicion with a credible 'selfish' justification. For example, 'How about if I throw in free shipping?' or 'If you make this sale, you have a chance to win a trip to Spain.'

Sharp Angle Close: in which the salesperson responds to a prospect question with a request to close. For example, 'If I can meet your request to have the new car delivered within two weeks, do we have a deal?'

Common Mistakes

There are some common mistakes while using the technique expressed above that result in unsuccessful sales, as follows:

- Tells instead of sells; doesn't ask enough questions. Open-ended questions are those where the answer can lead to another question. It is used to explore a prospect's mind. It starts with what, where, why, when, and how. Whereas a close-ended question has a one-word answer – usually a yes or no. It is used to extract specific information like name, age, etc.
- Over-controls the call by asking too many close-ended questions. Close-ended questions end up as an investigation rather than a conversation.
- Doesn't respond to customers' needs with benefits. Benefits are those that are valuable and personalized to the customers' desires and not arbitrary features.
- Doesn't recognize needs or gives benefits prematurely.
- Doesn't recognize or handle negative attitudes effectively.
- Makes weak closing statements or doesn't recognize when or how to close.

Chapter 7

The Age of Spirituality and the Customer

We have, consciously or subconsciously, searched for the answer to the question, 'What makes a person happy?'

While working smart and hard in our career, we should ask ourselves, 'Do we live to work or work to live?'

While making friends and investing in resources, we should ask ourselves, 'Do we invest to gain friends or gain friends to invest in a future favour?'

While extending our support to loved ones, we should ask, 'Do we love others for support, or do we support others for love?'

We realize that the ways we live do not bring 'happiness' in itself.

Even though all three areas of life are important for general existence, they are a means to an end and not the end itself. Yet it is not enough to be happy; we must share this with others. We were born into a society, and no person is an island. By sharing our happiness we correspondingly receive this in return by the limitless nature we live in. This makes most endeavours truly meaningful.

Happiness is a state of mind. The mind is a powerful part of us that has the ability to think rationally and creatively; it registers emotions and can recognize the emotions of others. The mind is the ignition of human behaviour. Our attitude is comprised of thoughts, emotions, and behaviours. When we generally claim to be happy, we actually claim to have the right attitude in all that we do.

In a nutshell, what makes a person happy is one's attitude:

- to flip our thoughts from negative to positive
- to find solutions to change our hostile emotions
- to act or behave in a constructive manner

We behave in a constructive manner when we address our thoughts (inclusive of emotions that are also in our thoughts). By this we realize happiness is a state of mind. Cynicism leaves us when happiness prevails. Finally, some questions seem meaningless and other questions meaningful when happiness prevails.

Flip Your Thoughts

Thoughts are rational and creative, and when the two meet they are a canvas for new ideas!

The mind has the capacity to archive thoughts in the subconscious only to reappear in the conscious for the future. Therefore, when you think, think 'real'! You can choose to think negatively and create a pseudo-reality, or you can think real and create abundance in reality! When you think of life as mere survival, you reduce yourself to basic instincts; however, when you think to overcome, endure, innovate, and succeed, you move a step beyond mere survival (and only a step) closer to your pure potential.

Your mind is linked to your anatomy, which means that when you are peaceful, the oxygen supply to your body is better, your heart rate is at the right speed, and your body is revitalized.

However, when you're nervous your body grudgingly absorbs oxygen to its cells, your heart rate is irregular, and your body is fatigued. Watch how you breathe and consciously change it for yourself. Consequently, you will discover what is actually on your mind as opposed to the rapid thoughts that fire through nervousness.

As you gain consciousness by simply breathing calmly you will be able to flip your thoughts from negative to positive. Most negative thoughts come from deep-rooted fears, which are expressed in reality with cynicism. You then expect the worst. Once you are conscious of simple breathing and make it as regular as you can, you ultimately behave in a different way in minor and major observations. For example, after an employer has made a thorough performance evaluation, you are called in for an interview for a new role, even a promotion. This interview could make you nervous. Flip your thoughts from cynicism – that is, stop asking yourself 'I wonder if I will get this role?' or saying, 'I don't care,' and flip to the constructive belief that 'I trust I will get this role because I care. If it is mutually the right fit, it will show.'

Flipping thoughts is not difficult to do. All it requires is your conscious attention to flip them, and over time they become habit, naturally flipping thoughts as your subconscious archives all thought alterations.

When you flip your thoughts, be flexible and ready to receive any result since we no longer expect the worst.

Coincidentally, we can face our human emotions and will them to change, either through conscious thoughts or from your subconscious archive. Either way, when thoughts and emotions change, your behaviour exudes agility rather than fatigue. Moreover, you are healthy and equipped to take on challenges.

Find Solutions for Hostile Emotions

We emote feelings, which in themselves are not wrong. Your reactions to those feelings are critical, especially if they are hostile. There is a fair deal of creativity hidden in emotions that come to the surface when emotions are expressed constructively. For example, you may feel angry about a certain circumstance that brought out deep-rooted fears through your subconscious that ignited hostile emotions. In such a case, walk away from the situation and resort to a constructive expression of a hostile emotion. This could be seeking any form of creation such as drawing, writing a poem or song, dancing, saying a prayer, or playing a sport. These expressions are constructive in relationships or circumstances.

Emotions such as anger, sadness, dispassion, and many more hostile feelings are not wrong, but it's wrong to act on them, especially toward others. Emotions such as happiness, ecstasy, passion, and many more are also not wrong to feel in themselves and are acceptable to act upon because they are fruitful to relationships and circumstances. Emotions, as a whole, are beautiful when used creatively.

When we use our creative emotions to overcome hostile ways they become constructive by mere creative action. Let hostile emotions inspire you towards creative and constructive expressions, void of cynicism in thought, only to release those hostile emotions without harm and with innovation. Emotions are priceless when used constructively. Don't hesitate to express creatively.

Finally, we are more than what we feel. This is a fact. Therefore, it is advisable to pick a career of creative expression if your emotions are a large part of who you are. Even if not a large part, pick a hobby to express your emotions creatively and constructively. All careers require a certain level of creative expression, some less and some more.

Behave in a Constructive Manner

What is the difference between a destructive and constructive manner? A destructive manner is to bring an end to all things that give life. A constructive manner is to logically create what gives life. We harness logic when we overturn irrational behaviour. To behave is to act out. To behave in a constructive manner is to act out logically for the creation of what gives life meaning.

What gives life meaning? Those activities that reform the self. As we address emotions with creation, we address behaviour with logic. Logic is what leads premise to a valid conclusion. Any argument must have a valid conclusion governed by logic. What is logical bears fruit through behaviour. What is illogical can rot good intentions with irrational behaviour. For example, why does a thief who consistently steals have no remorse? Because the thief gets so used to doing the wrong that it does not seem wrong after a certain point. The first theft would have been with discomfort since logic still existed, after that, logic dissolved in the illogical motivations in the act of theft leading to a lack of remorse.

Similarly, we act out certain times in unfavourable ways that are illogical to the receiver, yet we do this often enough to forget that they are unfavourable ways. We temporarily succeed in those ways. The success is temporary because it is rooted in irrationality and/or a destructive manner. Logical motivations lead to logical behaviour.

Finally, we behave how we think and feel. If we behave unfavourably, then we think illogically, and when we follow a destructive manner, we operate out of hostile emotions in its pure nature and not with creation. So for the overall health and wellness of self and society, it is suggested we think, feel, and behave in a constructive manner. Those who do not haven't consciously recognized the validity of change in their attitude. All people intrinsically must care for themselves and care to serve society; this should be enough inspiration to behave in a constructive manner

What Do You Want from Life?

We all have certain desires to fulfil, and at the least we observe the world around us for our own evolution. We have the tenacity to exist with the ability to think, feel, and act. What you think is what you will breed, so be cognisant of limitless possibilities, using the present moment for a great future. Don't lose the present moment, since once it passes it cannot be changed and can remain a memory.

Every second consists of the past, present, and future all at once. Our minds can comprehend this fact and have the capacity to be governed by time, thus by the principles of destiny. Our minds also have the capacity to be governed by timelessness, thus by the principles of eternity. Eternity is a state of timelessness. What you are doing at this point in time is destiny. Reality consists of both eternity and destiny, timelessness and time. Our goals lead us to our destiny while being mindful of eternity, and this ties spirituality to reality. The principles of eternity guide discernment in our lives, and the principles of destiny work with our ultimate decisions.

Life asks many questions of you. The main question it asks is, 'What do you want from life?'

Amongst the many questions it asks, life holds great promise to deliver, provided you are supportive of life's ways. Life is of a giving nature while it takes from you what you want to receive. This means that when you are negative in attitude, life gives you the negative that you put in. So when you are positive in attitude, life gives you the same.

This also may suggest that whatever happens to you is of your ownership. In a personal framework, if negativity prevails, then you allowed this. If you want life to give you peace, then acknowledge that peace does not arise from the external world. It is a personal disposition that arises from within you.

You are most peaceful when you

- accept the world around you; ending rejections within and around you;

- forgive the people who have hurt you, ending doubt and fear within and around you;
- take ownership of the part you have played, ending blame and regression within and around you;
- affirm all that is good in this world, ending misdirection within and around you; and
- recognize the purpose of the unfavourable things that happen with its lessons, ending aggression within and around you.

By this, life gradually gives you acceptance, forgiveness, ownership, affirmations, and purpose in return; these will lead you to peace in a personal framework. You eventually show this peace from within to the external world and receive this in return. The purpose of 'giving' is not 'taking', yet the law of nature returns all that you give in its wondrous ways from various resources, and not necessarily from the same resource you gave to. The good we receive regurgitates back into the external world and is an eternal cycle.

Similarly, you may want temporary delights from life, and you may even see those materialize, yet for the sake of your purpose in the long haul, it is better to desire the good than bad. 80 per cent good and 20 per cent bad does not make anything 100 per cent right. The battle in this world and within ourselves is of good and bad, right and wrong – to develop personally would require you to acknowledge the existence of these and work through good and bad, right and wrong for a bright future. Both have their place in the larger reality. We all may not be in a position to know their place in the larger reality, yet we have the ability to distinguish between the two and pursue what would be suited to our evolution and purpose for positive progression. Something that may be bad may be right to one and may be wrong to the other, as perception – there is truth that is singular in nature that needs to be pursued for the welfare of all people.

We realize that personal development is not confined to etiquette and attitude alone but also requires a moral understanding of good and bad, right and wrong for the greater good of this world.

Finally, since every second consists of the past, present, and future all at once, the vital question is what do you want from life?

Don't Quit

Don't give up on life, and you will not disappoint yourself and your Creator. Don't quit! Your life should be a celebrated responsibility to you. You celebrate with your heart and are the one responsible for your thoughts, feelings, and actions. The carnal self is motivated by the desires of the flesh, while spirituality for personal development is motivated by the desires of the conscience. Even though the constant battle within us is to win one over the other to adequately operate in the world.

There are numerous personalities, perspectives, and feelings within ourselves that can be contradictory, and some can be present simultaneously, plunging oneself into confusion. When the pursuit is of single-mindedness, then our mental representations of facts are most genuine and lead us towards discernment. This keeps us unbiased and open to understanding intentions, actions, and consequences. By this openness we have a greater ability to discern with eyes wide open and make correct decisions.

In the world we live in today, with everything we have been through, we have reached a point where we need to decide our individual approach to the future. Even though the world has faced unfortunate and terrifying disasters, it also has its successes. We require a need to harness successes with tolerance, especially when certain decisions may not be in our hands. Life is a serious matter, and as it is commonly said, 'Don't laugh *at* me, laugh *with* me.' Which means no person is worthy of our degradation – so why should we degrade? Some may feel that they don't mind being laughed at, which still will not make this deed desirable. In the end our account is not of how desirable we are but how tolerant we are and how tolerant we have been. Take on challenges, utilize your talent – that is what talent is there for and don't quit! Persist in what there is to 'know' and pursue progression.

How to Choose

To accept or to reject is a choice. The foolish accept everything and everyone around them. The wise discern. The conscious mind can choose to accept the good and reject the bad from a very personal perspective, which is from your conscience and from where your soul resides.

You can choose correctly with an integrated consciousness. An integrated consciousness shows a coherency and correlation amongst the three elements of attitude, which are thought, emotion, and behaviour, and this intertwines with being decision-oriented. As such your intentions are sound, your actions are favourable and show fidelity to your intention, and the consequence that you estimate indeed follows as the actual consequence.

To be decision-oriented is to run the three (intention, action, and consequence) in your thoughts to seek favourability, fidelity, and exactness. Making a decision in this manner leads you to be clear and accepting in thought, emotion, and behaviour. If you do not accept your thought, emotion, and/or behaviour, you should reject the decision you had intended to make because you can surely find better solutions.

Further, if the consequence was not similar to or the same as the consequence estimated, then the thought, emotion, and behaviour – before you made that decision – was incoherent and uncorrelated. Therefore, an integrated consciousness is one that can supply the correct direction to you.

You ultimately should choose to accept what does not degrade your mind, body, and soul. You are then a celebrated responsibility to yourself.

The spiritual age will be the quest of the human spirit to attain enlightenment. The satisfaction of information will be accessible too quickly, and this will drive the human person to seek contentment of a different kind. This will be the ignition of the spiritual age.

The human person engages in mental dialogue to satisfy the desire of self-comprehension. The spiritual age will enhance this mental dialogue into a deeper and more meaningful communication with the conscience instead and thus with the world. No more will a person seek the self to reach enlightenment; indeed, a person will seek what is greater than themselves as a means for spiritual enlightenment and will realize the self in the process.

Spirituality has always been present; however, our human tendency has been to ignore this. When we encounter anything, we identify and ascertain what we have encountered. By this we realize magnitude and draw great wisdom to serve and then realize the self. We can truly know how real the spiritual enlightenment is when we serve, for we act from our own free will then we 'know'.

The spiritual age will bring the human person down from the pedestal of grandiosity and assist mankind in realizing the humility and their driving force. Those who claim the human person does not have a choice are mistaken. Everyone is free to choose, and it may be the odds faced that give the illusion as lack of independent choice.

Absolute ideas may be deeply ingrained in human minds, but the acceptance of absolute ideas as one's own are only practiced with a conscious decision. This conscious decision is drawn from within the conscience where truth resides.

The desire for perfection will propel the age of spirituality, and this desire is sought after in current times. Since we are intrinsically aware of the role of spirituality in business for frontline professionals in the quest for perfection, let us be well prepared for it!

Finally, ideas such as 'consistency' and 'excellence' exist in their purest form in our minds whether we believe they do or not. By tapping into them we have the potential to express them in our external world. We endeavour to keep seeking them to fully realize our potential.

About the Author

Anchal Andrews was born on 2 March 1982. She started her education in Convent of Jesus and Mary, led by the Irish Nuns in New Delhi, India. She featured in the local news as a 'Whiz Kid in the Arts'. She has presented to an audience of fifteen thousand fans and has been recognised by the Biglions Society Award.

As a student, Anchal won 15 certificates, seven trophies, and even gold medals for her contributions to the arts in UAE. She secured the Environmental Action Award by the Emirates Environmental Group, as well as a leading position in the Dubai Shopping Festival amongst leading artists. For her vocational pursuits, she extended her services to Al Noor and DCSN – schools for special needs. Anchal travelled to Toronto, Canada, and performed for the Toronto Music Festival. She was an advanced student in the leading performance art and fine arts school in Canada at the time. She studied and secured 78 per cent as marks in school, and she was a consistent star performer. She volunteered at Larsche, a school for special-needs students, while studying psychology in Saint Francis Xavier University in Antigonish, Nova Scotia, Canada.

She was elected minister of the Roman Catholic Church and served post-confirmation. She returned to UAE and continued her career in sales-and-service training and development. After fifteen years she started a training and development company in 2013 to predominantly lead frontline professionals. Since January 2014 she has trained more than a thousand participants with a 97 per cent positive evaluation rate.

Anchal Andrews continues in training and development for sales and service. As any good leader, she has vision for the long term that she believes will be accomplished. Her career began at age sixteen, in Canada, when she already knew that she would own a successful business in training and development someday. Anchal centred her career options on this goal ever since. She began the journey as a telemarketer, when she gained the relevant experience to lead a skill-sets training services company within the industries of financial services, banking, and the automotive industry. She has trained and developed staff in every institution she has worked in and has been trained in best practices in leadership. The work experience she gained has been the mould that has made her a 'star performer' consistently. She thrives on developing knowledge, skills, and a positive attitude.

She has gone through extreme lengths to understand the relevance of spirituality and its existential connection with sales and customer service. Anchal has undergone various experiences and has proven that this approach delivers results, as adopted in large organizations and SMEs. This approach requires leaders and frontline professionals to participative to deliver results.

This can be a one-man-practice and has proven to be a great team approach to customer service and sales.

Anchal has researched religions; spirituality of religions; secular spirituality; customer service–applied skills; sales-applied skills; and leadership. She translated various ideas into practices, and this propelled her forward.

She integrates ancient and current practices in an approach she calls *Beyond Frontline Excellence*.